I0149145

All Scripture references taken from the KJV of the Holy Bible, unless otherwise indicated.

EVIL PETITION in the COURT of ACCUSATION by Dr. Marlene Miles

Freshwater Press, 2023

ISBN: 978-1-960150-71-4

Contents

Evil Petition

in the

Court of Accusation

Freshwater

Then he showed me Joshua the high priest

standing before the angel of the Lord,

and Satan standing at his right side

to accuse him.

(Zechariah 3:1)

Waiting to Accuse

Have you ever gone through periods of time where things are not going right, and you can't really understand why? Have you had seasons in your life where you feel that things are up against you, but you haven't done anything that you know of to cause it? Does it sometimes seem that invisible forces are working against you to make your life difficult, complicated, or sometimes impossible? Does it feel like you are fighting a battle, but it is an invisible battle?

Chances are very good that you are not imagining things. Things that are simple and should be straightforward are not. Simple things are hard. Sometimes it appears that disaster strikes out of the blue.

Yes, there is a whole invisible spirit world and if you don't have control and take authority over all the parts of your life, the players of that elusive world will try to move the chess pieces on the board of your life.

I want us to think for a while about the story of Job, and how the devil wanted to do bad things to Job.

Do you think Job foresaw any of that disaster that beset him and his family? Do you think Job had an inkling or a clue that fierce storms were brewing? Not much unlike the catastrophic insurance commercials we see on TV, life comes at folks. The evil in the spirit world influences the evil people in our natural world to do things to people—even good people. Sometimes, they especially do bad things to good people, or people who are trying to be good.

But while Job was going through trials and tribulations and testing by the hand of the devil, God had to tell the devil not to kill Job. If God had to say that to the devil, then God already knew that's what the devil wanted to do. The devil hates man, not just Job. The devil hates mankind.

God allowed the devil to give Job boils, because the devil believed that Job would curse

God, but Job did not. Satan took out **ALL** 10 of Job's original first 10 children and I suppose some or all of them had spouses and maybe, also children. The devil just killed them; he doesn't care. He comes to STEAL. KILL. DESTROY.

We need to be aware of his tactics all the time. We need to be wise. We need to always be learning, and always alert, in the Name of Jesus.

Job was an upright man before God—and you may be and upright man before God, as well--, we all want to think that we are. But for the devil to get permission to accost Job, there seems to have been an Evil Petition presented in Heaven. The purpose of an Evil Petition is to get a judgment against a man, and then the devil can start his steal, kill and destroy activities against that man. As far as the devil is concerned, this judgment is permission to do his thing against mankind, the group he hates so much.

Man has been given authority and dominion over all the works of God's hands and that includes the scorpion, the serpent and ALL the power of the enemy. Get that–, **ALL** the power of the enemy. Remember that, please.

Behold, I give you the authority to trample on serpents and scorpions, and over all the power of the enemy, and nothing shall by any means hurt you. (Luke 10:19)

So really, we are supposed to be the boss of the devil. But, like any bad worker, the devil wants to stick it to *the man--*, literally, all mankind. If we don't know **we are the boss** and take our rightful positions the devil will try and can run all over us.

In order for the devil to do harm to Job, or any of us, he needs to get permission from God. We are protected by God but if we step out of authority and out of position then we lose the protection of God. For Job to be vulnerable there had to be something missing, lacking, wrong with Job, in Job, about Job or sinful about Job. This missing thing would be the result of sin, and that must have been hidden to the reader and also to Job the reason the devil was allowed to do horrible, devastating things to Job.

The devil will bring an Evil Petition up before the Lord against you, against anyone that he can, to get a judgment and condemnation to steal, kill and destroy. Ruining the man's life, destiny --, everything. This is a serious word for your life and wellbeing.

Satan got a hold of Job because he went up to Heaven and *asked.* In a sense, God was bragging on Job when He said, ***"Have you seen my servant, Job?"*** The devil took that as a challenge to show God that Job wasn't *all that.* The devil didn't try to prove that Job would sin outrightly, because Job didn't sin overtly. Instead the devil set but to prove that Job's **heart position** would be found lacking in times of trouble. Remember, God judges man by his **heart**, not necessarily what he does in church, or what he *looks like* in public.

Satan is the accuser of the brethren and he probably accused Job of something or several things. Whether the accusation was true or not, we don't know because there is no record or indication in that Book of Scripture that Job went up to the Courts of Heaven and ***answered*** an Evil Petition brought by Satan.

That is the gist of this book, to tell that Evil Petitions brought into the Court of Accusation, also called the Court of Petition, and how we as

Christians must handle ourselves when this is our case.

The answer is that we need to **answer** Evil Petitions so that judgments are not gotten against us in the Spirit, so we are not ambushed by evil and so that our life will go well.

And I heard a loud voice saying in heaven, Now is come salvation, and strength and the kingdom of our God, and the power of His Christ: for the accuser of our brethren is cast down, which accused them before our God day and night.
(Revelations 12:10)

The devil will stand at the throne of God – there is more than one throne, in Heaven, but we are talking about the Throne of Petition or the Throne of Accusation in this book. The devil will stand there and accuse man day and night. That would be 24/7. If he himself is not there, his representatives will be there to accuse day and night. That's a lot of accusing.

Why do you think he is doing all this accusing at the Throne of God?

The devil doesn't just want to accuse a man so that man will get in trouble with God. The devil wants to **BE** that trouble that man gets into. He wants to steal from that man, kill him, if possible and destroy his life, purpose, ministry, destiny, his whole family--, his bloodline. Just look at what he did to Job; he decimated the man's family and life!

The devil starts out with just an accusation, as in a court of law to try to get a judgment against a man that he may steal, kill, destroy him, **if the judgment stands.**

The devil in the New Testament had Pharisees accusing Jesus. What do you think the devil is saying to God about *you* if the devil has the nerve to *accuse* **Jesus**? Pharisees were employed by Satan--, in return for being evil to Jesus, the Pharisees kept their prominent *religious* positions as they served the "god of this world" while looking like they were serving Jehovah God. Saints of God, that still happens today. **Try every spirit.**

The Pharisees kept looking for things to accuse Jesus of to take Him to natural court, put Him and jail and, of course, eventually to do away with Him.

Evil Petition is very serious, and it seems no one is exempt. Don't lose heart, the only reason the Pharisees succeeded against Jesus as it was in the plan of God. The Lord has put protections in for His people, there is a way of escape when Evil Petitions are filed against you in the Court of Accusation.

Fair warning here, the accusations against you by the devil to God in the Court of Petition or Accusation, may **not** be false; they may be true. Even though the devil is a liar and the father of lies, he knows if he wants to get anywhere with God he'd better come with some truth--, he'd better come with the goods. This is why *monitoring spirits* and *familiar spirits* watch you, since birth to give reports and also to help present temptations to you so you will sin. Even sins where you think nobody saw and nobody will know are seen by evil entities that report their findings into their network of evil to get you accused before God, if at all possible.

Where do you think people get the idea to accuse, or falsely accuse others? The devil. He is the accuser, and he's a liar. What he's counting on with Evil Petition is **that you won't be there** to answer for yourself. If you are the type to procrastinate, not do things you should do on time or at all – *familiar spirits* know this. You're a good candidate to be accused of something and you'll do nothing about it. If you're prayerless, careless, or don't believe in all that *stuff* – you're the one they will choose. If you are one to not even open your mail or handle the details of your natural life, then you might become a spiritual victim of the devil for not handling *spiritual* business and *spiritual* details.

<u>You</u> are expected to be in the Spirit, in worship, in prayer, and in the Courts of the Lord especially if there is a live Petition against you there. Yes, Jesus is our High Priest, He is our Advocate and our Intercessor, but some things we have to do ourselves. We have to be there and answer to God, ourselves.

The devil is counting on you not being there. If you are not there you default, it's a forfeit, as a baseball game that you don't show up for--, how will you win? Even though you may have the best team, you have to be present to win.

With Jesus as our Advocate, He's never lost a battle, so we will win with Him. Always. Accusations are coming up in Evil Petitions, even if you are accused falsely, if you're not there--, too bad for you.

The Pharisees wanted to accuse Jesus so badly because they had taken on the *nature* of their idol. We all do, actually. Satan was their idol, so they were acting just like the devil, accusing the brethren. They didn't realize that Satan had seduced them and entered into them. They thought they were holy and righteous, but they had actually taken on the nature of Satan and the spirit of the anti-Christ. They were constantly looking for something to accuse Jesus about. They wanted to kill the man, destroy Him--, day and night. The devil wants **gotcha** moments against man so that he can feel that he's won.

Yeah, people really do take on the nature of their idols, their demons. You don't have any demons, do you? Then everything you do should be in the nature of Christ.

Is it?

So, Satan accuses man day and night; he really wants to condemn man. Steal from him, kill and destroy man, make his life worthless. He starts by accusing, day and night. He wants gotcha moments trying to get God to condemn His own creation. But our God is full of love and tender mercies toward us; every morning new mercies.

Satan has access to the Courts of Heaven, but so do we. Have you been there? Have any of us been there? We have access.

Through satanic accusations if he wins, if he prevails he can torment man, he could kill, he could steal. To counter this **WE** must appear at this evil petition so we can be victorious so that the things that we are going through because of the Evil Petition can be shut down, or the judgment can be reversed.

The Spirit is not tied to time and space like flesh is, so we can go there right now, it's not like when you miss a court date in the natural. You may be going through things in the natural, torments, or losses and you realize that something is not right. You might be saying,

What God promised me I'm not getting it; I'm getting the opposite of that. There must be some Evil Petitions in the Courts of Heaven against me – so I'm going there.

So you get into prayer, you get into the Spirit with God, in worship and you can go into the Courts of Heaven. We appear at the Court and we address the Evil Petition, when we are victorious then we can see a **sudden reversal of the symptoms** of evil, thievery, and theft in our lives. This adds structure to that *suddenly* of God that we've read about for years.

Let all mine enemies be ashamed and sore vexed: let them return [and] be ashamed suddenly. (Psalm 6:10)

None of us like to be in front of nosey neighbors and prying eyes. **The nosiest is the devil.** He is forever looking at you, looking into what you're doing. He is not Omnipresent like God, so he sends *monitoring spirits* who are constantly spying to see what you've done and what you are doing or planning. *Monitoring spirits* report back to the devil and their reports even include when it's a good time to attack you--, if you have *unguarded hours.*

The devil is always looking for something to accuse you to God. And if you are a sinner, don't think no one saw it. *Someone* or some entity is looking; somebody saw it. You didn't get away with it—accusations could be in the works against you right now because of that sin. That something could be as formal as an Evil Petition in the Courts of Petition or Accusation right now.

The devil is brazen; even if he, *himself* incited you to do the sin, he will still accuse you as if he had nothing to do with it. Entrapment is not beyond the scope of his activities. He will entice you to do a sin and then run and tell that.

If you *feel accused* and no one around you actually pointing a finger at you, that's most likely a spiritual thing you're feeling. It's the devil. You're picking up on something that is happening in the Spirit; you are not crazy, you are *spiritual.* Thank God.

Satan is a legalist, he is continually looking for any fault in any man, any of us, to use to accuse us before God. Once he has an accusation against a man, then the Court of Accusation (Court of Petition) is convened to hear the charges. Saints of God, we *must* go, we must respond. Period. We must respond. We must go for ourselves, we can't just send someone for us, although Jesus will be with us, Amen.

Will You Pray For Me?

People often ask others, *Will you pray for me?* This is one time where we can't send someone for us. Sometimes in this life we do need prayer support. We know that one praying soul will put 1000 angels to flight and two will put 10,000 to flight; corporate prayer is powerful, but you have to go yourself to this Court.

And this is how to do it:

The spirit of man can engage the spiritual realm at any time, including the realms of Heaven. Jesus said that He is the Door. And, He said that wherever IIe is we may be there also. Not just for eternity and the end times, but this is for now. So, if we go by Jesus Christ, the Door, we can get into these Courts. We need to get into Courts where there may be Evil Petitions with our name on it.

Feelings and promptings of being **accused** should prompt us to appear in Heavenly Courts to inquire about and answer Evil Petitions that may be up against you. God may speak to you in dreams, and again you need proper, correct, Christian, Biblical dream interpretation. When you see a throne in your dream, get up to the Heavenly Courts and see if there is an Evil Petition against you. If you see people around a Throne in your dream, get to the Court of Accusation. If you see odd looking people, even dark or evil looking people around a throne, especially--, get up there.

If you have a dream of someone chasing you with a weapon, Evil Petitions could be secretly being presented against you. The devil may be trying to get permission to steal from you, hurt you, or even kill you.

As I said, it may not be the devil himself, but a representative. There are evil human agents who won't mind acting out evil against another human, especially a Christian. Some love to do evil, so you **must** stay prayed up.

If there is a promise that the Lord has made to you but there seems to be an obstacle to you receiving it, your blessing could have been subverted, hijacked or snatched from you by an Evil Petition and by a judgment rendered that you don't know anything about. You may need to go to Court and learn something about it.

We're watching TV--, The People's Court, Judge Judy, Divorce Court, Judge *this*, Judge *that*--, NO! Heavenly Courts are NOT for your entertainment; this is for your real LIFE. The things that pertain to your peace, the things that allow you to possess your possessions, the things that allow you to have all things for life and for godliness, hinge on how you live before the Lord. If you repent when you sin, and if you will have the spiritual acuity to understand that there may be an Evil Petition in the Heavens against you, and your willingness to answer it will determine a lot of your success in this life. You deserve to have the life that Jesus came here and died for you to have.

Get yourself to *spiritual* court, at the Throne of God in the heavenlies. There, you must answer any Evil Petition that is up there against you. Amen.

There is more than one Court in Heaven, we do not have access to all of them immediately, but the Court of Accusation, also called the Court of Petition –, everyone has access to it.

You need to see the Judge, you need to stand in front of that Judge, the Judge of the entire universe, the Righteous Judge.

Get yourself to this Court and look to see if your name is on the docket. **Seriously,** go into the spirit and ASK God, *Is there an accusation, are there accusations up here against me?*

Chances are you will get an immediate answer either in words, understanding, or a vision of some kind. Ask who. Ask why. Ask to see the charges.

Saints of GOD, have no fear. We bind and paralyze the *spirit of fear* because God has not given us the *spirit of fear* but one of Love, Power, and a sound mind. Have no fear as to what you *may* see when you go there. Have no fear as to what you may *hear* while you are there. No fear as to what you may experience because you are going by the Door; you are going with Jesus Christ, He is with you. He will not leave you.

Ask or look to see if your name is on the Docket. Ask something like, *Is there anyithing against me, Lord?*

You may want to put that question in the form of symptoms and situations. *Lord, I'm going through lack, loss or poverty right now, is it because of an Evil Petition against me, or a judgment that has been rendered against me?*

You may inquire because of pain or sickness in the body, ask the same thing, *Is there an Evil Petition, an accusation against me, Lord?*

Lord, why am I not married, or enjoying my marriage that I'm in? Lord, why don't I have children? Lord, why do I suffer rejection on the job and have never gotten a work promotion?

And so on…Just **ask** God.

Ask, and it shall be given you; seek, and ye shall find; knock, and it shall be opened unto you: (Matthew 7:7)

Think in terms of court, specifically in the Courts of Petition when we get there, we **ask**. We find out what the charges or the accusations are. We **ask** for the book or the documents that show the infringement (sin), and that book (scroll) shall be opened for us to see.

The Word of God has everything we need for every situation, even today, although the Bible was penned so many hundred years ago. The Words of the Bible are not mere words, they are *Spirit* therefore they transcend space and time. So ask, seek, find, knock and it shall be opened to you, even in the Court of Petition.

Not Evil Councils

Dear Reader, I must clarify here that the Courts of Heaven and any of the Thrones of God are **not** the same as any evil mock court or evil council meetings that are held at vairious and sometimes in undisclosed locations throughout the world, spiritually and physically speaking. At Evil Council meetings, and also in covens and hives, people are discussed and are often, *in absentia*, put on trial by entities or evil human persecutors. There, evil verdicts, witchcraft verdicts are issued against also unsuspecting people --, even the saints of God--, sometimes especially the saints of God. But know, that is a thing.

There are numerous Evil Councils, I obtained this overview list from Bride Ministries, compiled by Dr. Daniel Duval. Seek that site for more information and prayers to be delivered from Evil Councils.

According to Duvall, every Council listed here has been confirmed through an actual deliverance. The site offers a disclaimer: *"Please keep in mind that this list is not all-inclusive, as we continue to run into new Evil Councils all the time."*

Through deliverances, that ministry has uncovered ten **Councils of 13 which I will not enumerate or discuss their locations. Other Councils are:** the Council of 3, the Council of 7, the Council of 11, the Council of 80, and 13 other Councils which are named by their location. None of that is in the scope of this book. Additionally, there are **Luminary Councils, Synthetic Councils, AI Council, Alien Group Councils. Occult Councils, Earth Councils,** for every nation on Earth, and there are at least two named **Military Base Councils.**

https://deliverance.bridemovement.com/resourc e-page/evil-councils/

Just confirming, the Court of Petition/ the Court of Accusation is in the Spirit realm. It involves God as the Righteous Judge and Jesus Christ as the Christian victim's advocate. The above named Councils are not that, they are only included in this book as an FYI.

Now, back to our regularly scheduled program:

Courts of the Lord

Learning about Heavenly Courts adds new meaning to the Courts of the Lord, *right*? God holds court. There are multiple throne rooms, Yes we know the Throne of Grace, because we are invited to go there, and ask for Mercy and Grace in times of trouble.

Let us therefore come boldly unto the throne of grace, that we may obtain mercy, and find grace to help in time of need, (Hebrews 4:16)

Particularly there is a Throne of Accusation or Petition. This is where the devil and his cohorts come to bring accusations and Evil Petitions against a man. They can't do the bad things they want to do against a person until they get permission. Recall, what may have happened to Job was that a judgment may have been issued against him, giving the devil permission to touch Job's family, abundance, provision, and life.

Then he showed me Joshua the high priest standing before the angel of the Lord, and Satan standing at his right side to accuse him,
(Zechariah 3:1)

Satan was standing at the right side of the high priest, Joshua to accuse him. By this we know that even the high priest is not immune to demonic accusation and attack, if it is allowed.

The Pharisees were constantly looking for something of which to **ACCUSE** Jesus.

Where the Word of God says, *Agree with thine adversary quickly, lest he turn you over to the Judge* is found in Matthew 5:25.

Agree with thine adversary quickly, whiles thou art in the way with him; lest at any time the adversary deliver thee to the judge, and the judge deliver thee to the officer, and thou be cast into prison. (Matthew 5:25)

In the scheme of things of the Spirit, you can see the adversary as a roaring lion seeking prey.

Be alert and of sober mind. Your enemy the devil prowls around like a roaring lion looking for someone to devour.(1 Peter 5:8 NIV)

Stay alert! Watch out for your great enemy, the devil. He prowls around like a roaring lion, looking for someone to devour. (1 Peter 5:8 NLT)

This roaring lion, the devil, desires to deliver a man to the Judge--, that would be God. If you aren't there to answer the Petition, then the devil may win a judgment against his victim. If the judgment is obtained then you are delivered to the *officer*, which could be a strongman or any demon that is assigned to enforce the judgment against you. If you are cast into prison, that is **spiritual captivity.** Once in captivity, the jailer/strongman can do anything he wants to you, either forever, until death, or just for a season.

That's complicated you may say. Yes, it is. If the devil captures a human, he wants to make it difficult to impossible for him to get away from jail or captivity.

Still we have hope. While there is life there is hope. The Lord has promised to not leave our souls in hell; He has promised to turn our captivity. But we have to know that we are captive first and then know how to be delivered from the jailer, the strongman, the devils and his henchmen. Read my book: **Souls in Captivity** There are extensive prayers at the back of my books to remedy the problem discussed in the book itself. https://a.co/d/1JaFV2p

So we agree with the adversary quickly so he doesn't accuse you and bring an Evil Petition up against you. There must be balance here. This does not mean that you agree with an attacking adversary who is at that very moment threatening your life, the life of your family, or the things over which you have stewardship. This means that if you are accused and you're in Court because the Court has convened to hear the accusation, **AGREE** with the accusation quickly as you are before the Righteous Judge, with Jesus is your Advocate.

This Court case will be heard, with or without you. But if you are there, agree in the proceedings.

There seems to be no record that Job went to a Court to answer the accusation(s). This is spiritual court, so it would be impossible for Job to agree quickly, or at all, even with wise and powerful Counsel by his side if Job didn't go to Court. Of course, we know throughout the Book of Job that everyone thought that **God** did all these things to Job, not the devil. So that's certainly a problem if you also think like that.

The Prophet Zechariah shows us something altogether different, however.

Then he showed me Joshua the high priest standing before the angel of the Lord, and Satan standing at his right hand to accuse him.
2 And the Lord said to Satan, *"The Lord rebuke you, O Satan! The Lord who has chosen Jerusalem rebuke you! Is not this a brand plucked from the fire?"*
3 Now Joshua was standing before the angel, clothed with filthy garments.

4 And the angel said to those who were standing before him, *"Remove the filthy garments from him."* And to him he said, *"Behold, I have taken your iniquity away from you, and I will clothe you with pure vestments."*
5 And I said, *"Let them put a clean turban on his head."* So they put a clean turban on his head and clothed him with garments. And the angel of the Lord was standing by.
(Zechariah 3:1-5, ESV)

Joshua was standing before the Lord in filthy garments; and that is exactly what we are wearing as a result of **sin**. That is not how we were created, though; we were created in the image and likeness of God. GOD IS NOT DEFILED. Sin is defilement and it undoes a lot of good. Dirty or soiled garments, even in the dream, are an indication of defilement. So, Joshua in dirty garments indicates that there must have been some truth to the impending accusation.

The Devil will entrap, snare, trick, lead and urge, incite and invite you to sin. That's when your beautiful garment of righteousness that the Lord has given you, becomes stained, soiled, dirty--, even filthy. Sin puts an evil garment on you, DECLARING YOU GUILTY and fit for judgment and condemnation.

In Bible days what garment your wore stated your station in life. In the Spirit what you are wearing indicates your spiritual station and status.

Joshua, the High Priest presented before the Lord in a soiled garment, but God said, **Take off that filthy garment, I'm going to put a clean garment on you**. This is the Lord saying that even though there was sin, because of the Blood of Jesus, I'm taking this evil garment off of you and I am declaring you, **NOT GUILTY**. You are not going to be condemned.

And his raiment became shining, exceeding white as snow; so as no fuller on earth can white them. (Mark 9:3)

He that overcometh, the same shall be clothed in white raiment; and I will not blot out his name out of the book of life, but I will confess his name before my Father, and before his angels.
(Revelation 3:5)

But while in the filthy garment, the devil is trying to declare you Guilty and make you fit for judgment and condemnation. God hates defilement. He hates sin and is very particular about our righteousness.

God says, **Remove the filthy garments from him. Behold, I have taken your iniquity away and I will clothe you with pure vestments**.

Joshua was given a clean garment, and that was the garment of righteousness which we get by the Blood of Jesus and God imputing the righteousness of Jesus to us, to declare us **NOT GUILTY**, in the Name of Jesus.

No Time to Waste

Woe to those who are at ease in Zion – those who think the devil is not bothering you so you have nothing to do, spiritually speaking. Those of you who think life is perfect and nothing is wrong, I want you to think of the worst "friend" that you've ever had in your life.

If Jesus is a friend that sticks closer than a brother, then the devil is the opposite.

This worst friend in the world/the universe will smile in your face, all the while they want to take your place; they are backstabbers. If this person gets into any trouble, or they may not like how great your life is going, they may just decide to ACCUSE you, even falsely, or maybe justly because if you two were friends, you may have confided a sin in them.

Or this fake friend may try to accuse you if *they* get into any trouble. They may try to escape trouble by dumping it all on you and say you made them do it. They could even take it to the level of saying that they wouldn't have done it at all if it weren't for you. And the absolute – *Look what you did. They will tell on you unprovoked…if it means saving their hide.*

In the Garden at Eden, Adam had taken on the nature of Satan when he said to God, *"That woman you gave me, made me eat."* Adam had become an accuser, like that Old Serpent.

We don't confide sin to the devil, but most often he's there because he's the one inviting, urging you to sin in the first place. So, with the devil – the THING that you did is most likely, TRUE if he is accusing you. The devil is a legalist and a stickler for the rules that **you** must follow. Whether you know the rules or not. Whether you even know that there are rules. And yes, there are rules, God's rules. So for all of you who think there is nothing on this Earth to do, there is. Plenty.

For all of you who think when you get to Heaven you will just sit on a cloud and play a harp – do you even know how to play a harp? Are you preparing for that? Are you taking harp lessons, just in case it's true? Well it's not true anyway. So don't just think you can live a life of ease here on Earth now that you're saved. Woe to those who are at ease in Zion.

You could be the object, the person named in an Evil Petition, not just once, but multiple times in your life and even in your Christian walk. There you are in the Spirit being accused and you may know nothing about it. You may be accused of things that you thought about, or thought up, even though the thought was actually presented *to* you, and you only considered it for a moment--, but you didn't even do it! You didn't *do* the sin. But thinking on a sin is still sin, especially lusting--, it is still sin.

You could be accused of the things you actually did, (the transgression) even though you were enticed, or invited, initiated, even dragged into *doing* the sin.

Don't Take the Dare

Growing up, one of my three older brothers would dare, even double dare me to do wrong things. He was relentless, so eventually I would accept his dares because I was like 8 years old – naïve. But the moment I did them, he would run and report to Dad exactly what I had just done. I'm not proud of this now, but I was a child, and I'm thinking, this is my brother, who made this dare with a smile on his face. I was thinking we were having fun and this was a game of some sort. But he'd tell on me right away.

I'm not proud of this, but I'm telling you this for a reason. I was a kid--, unregenerated. My brother had convinced me that this is something fun to do and I'm doing it. Beware of the person who invites you to do something wrong as if it's a joke and then go and accuse you to higher ups.

Unfortunately, at eight years old, I became very adept at getting out of trouble – too good at looking innocent in front of Dad, when I had done the crime that my brother had challenged me to do – telling me that I was too *chicken* to do. I can't believe my brother had betrayed me and now I have to figure out how not to get in trouble over this. I'm trying to appear innocent in front of Dad, when I actually had **done** the crime.

The devil is not your friend, neither is he your brother. He will also entice or dare you to sin and then make a beeline to God to accuse you.

My brother's challenges and the resultant crimes were childish, stupid things like stealing a quarter from the dresser – Dad's change that he had left there while in the bathroom taking the longest bath in America. Dad's change was on the dresser in his (my parents') own bedroom. I would go in there and take that quarter and then I would show my brother that I had the quarter. As soon as Dad came out of the bathroom, my brother would tattle. I would hide the crime. I said nothing, so I didn't lie verbally, but I would not show the quarter.

Don't do that.

That's not how it works with God. Recall, I was an unregenerated, 8-year-old, then. That's not how it works with God or in the Courts of Heaven. If you did something, confess it. If you sinned, repent of it. You don't try to trick God or wiggle your way out of crimes and sins, that is not how it works in the Spirit.

If you're a parent you know exactly what I am saying. For example, your kid could have eaten the last cookie and is fibbing about it. Or, he hit his brother. He's guilty and you are just waiting for your child to own it—confess, already. You know you will forgive them and move on because you are the parent. But when they stand their ground and double down on their sin, their crime, their lie, and the evil that they've done by lying or denying, you take an entirely different stance. Well, God is more like that.

You know you will forgive your own child.

What--, you think you won't? You will. You do not plan to kick your kid out of the family. Some evil parents do, but God doesn't do that either. Well, He doesn't do that unless a person really keeps sinning, sinning, sinning, has no conscience, is hurting others and has no heart of repentance and God knows they are reprobate and will never repent.

Parents: it is SO bad to let your child get away with things and not learn that it is better to tell the truth, 'fess up and own it and let's move on with things. That is how it works in the Kingdom of Heaven; it will be so much easier for them as adults if they learn that lesson early.

I'm speaking for myself here too: be quick. be transparent. To be in the Kingdom of God, be forthright. Be quick to own the sin, and then disown it. OWN it quickly by confessing that you did it. Then, disown it by repenting and giving it to **Jesus and the Lord will blot it out with the Blood of Jesus.**

In the process, you must also learn to forgive yourself.

As a follow up to the brother daring me story, I fell for his dare to get me in trouble only once. Amen.

How Long Does it Take to Repent?

In the past God overlooked such ignorance, but now he commands all people everywhere to repent. (Acts 17:30 NIV)

The Word of God says it is good for man to repent. God is not interested in how clever you are to try to get yourself out of trouble with Him, especially when you **did it**. It is good that we repent.

This is what the Lord shared with me regarding repentance. The Holy Spirit presented the question to me: **How long does it take to** *repent*?

A lot of people think they can just live their lives, do whatever they want 23/7 or 23.9/7 hours of the day and then when it's time to *go* --, somehow they think they will just know that it's time to *go* and quickly repent-- right then. What if you can't repent in two minutes or one minute, or *no* minutes? What if you can't repent in an hour? What if it takes you a long time to repent? **I've never known anyone to say that to repent is on their bucket list**. However, the Word says that it is good that man should repent.

How long do you think it'll take you to remember all the stuff that you did in your life up to this point, in order to repent? Do you think you can just blanket it and say, *Lord I repent of everything?*

With Godly sorrow you repent of things one by one, you name them. How long do you think it will take to repent? We may need to learn to repent. God loves a repentant heart; He loves a contrite spirit; He will hear that and will have Mercy on that kind of heart. If you automatically knew how to repent, you would have already repented--, you wouldn't be waiting until the last hour or moment or second. So obviously you'll have to **learn** how to repent.

The Word says that it is right and good that men repent, after all, we all have sinned and fallen short of the glory of God.

For all have sinned and come short of the glory of God, (Romans 3:23).

It may seem as though there is something to repent for. If there weren't why would we need *New* Mercies every day? Why would we need Mercy everyday unless something happened yesterday, or overnight while we slept--, even in the dream, while we are really *in the Spirit*?

When was the last time you repented? If you're supposed to be repenting every day, and there's at least one thing a day you need to repent of, but probably multiple things in a day. Let's say there's only one thing in a day you need to repent for. Can you identify what it is? What is that sin that you've committed? If you can't even identify it, you may not think it's sin, so you may be committing it every day. I don't know what your sin may be, but do you? The Holy Spirit will tell you and bring you under conviction. So let's say it's only one--, still that's 365 things in a year that a person may need to repent for. Have you repented for 365 things in the past year?

How long does it take to repent for 365 things? Not a minute. Not a second. Maybe not even in an hour can you repent of all those things. **How long does it take to *identify* those 365 things to repent for and then repent?**

How many *years* has it been since you repented? How long do you think it'll take you to repent for years and years of *not* repenting? It is not wise to live too close to the edge and think that at the last second, you're going to be able to repent to God and you'll be alright and just be in Heaven.

If you're stubborn enough to say that you are not going to repent until the last moment, that you've going to get all you can out of life, thinking that at the last moment, you'll know and have enough time to repent to God, properly, you may be sorely disappointed. In account after account of people who say they have seen Hell, the lament of everyone there seems to be they'd like to return to Earth, to **REPENT**. But by the time they are in hell, it is too late.

What if there are *people* in this life that you also need to repent to? God is Omnipresent, He is always there, but if there are people that you need to make amends with, when will you see them in that minute, or hour, or second?

I was listening to an actual minister of the Gospel who seeks the Lord, prays daily, seeks the face of God, and even sees signs and wonders in his ministry. It was a wonderful message. He said the Lord came to him and told him that if the world had ended last night that this minister would NOT have been taken to Heaven. Instead, he would have gone to Hell. An upright man, serving the Lord—, in Hell. It is unthinkable, isn't it?

Shocked, stunned, trembling and afraid – this minister sought the Lord for many hours that particular day to inquire as to why he would not have made Heaven. The Lord indicated to him that he needed to repent. This confused the man, after all, he wasn't actively sinning. So, repent *for what?*

He then said that the Lord took him back through his life, and showed him point by point, moment by moment, things that he did that were ungodly, that he thought no one else ever knew, that were left unrepented for. This was not a

Court of Accusation, but were these charges true? Of course they were, this was Jesus and Jesus does not lie.

From then, this pastor went on a sabbatical or retreat for a week or longer. I believe he was fasting as well. **And he repented for a week, or more.** Finally he felt as though he got a release from the Lord that he had repented for everything up to that point.

Truly, these times of ignorance God overlooked, but now commands all men everywhere to repent, (Acts 17:20 NKJV)

Immediate prayer:

Lord, in the Name of Jesus, I repent of all childhood dares and games, rebellion, disobedience, sin, crimes, sneaking, lying, and stealing. I especially repent of stealing that quarter from my Dad and then also not owning up to it. Lord, please forgive me. It was never in my heart to be a child to grieve either of my parents.

I turn from my wicked ways. Father, please forgive me for disrespecting or dishonoring my parents—both father and mother, in any way and release me from the curse of dishonoring parents. Lord, with this repentance, break the curse of dishonoring father or mother if that is over me, in the Name of Jesus.

Lord, I bind and paralyze every demon on assignment to enforce that curse. I break every bondage and yoke involved with the curse and any evil covenant created to let this curse even be in existence, by the Blood of Jesus.

Lord, remember this sin no more, but remember the times that I did honor mother and father and account that to me, so it will be well with me and I will have length of days on this Earth.

Lord, I am guilty, and I plead the Blood of Jesus, please cleanse me from all unrighteousness and give me a verdict of **NOT GUILTY** and a white, unsoiled robe of righteousness. In the Name of Jesus, I pray.

Lord, I hold nothing against my brother, forgive him also, in the Name of Jesus. **Amen.**

Seeking Deliverance

That prayer was repentance for something I did when I was 8 years old. It took me until this book to really remember it. How could I have repented for it before I fully recalled it?

How long does it take to repent?

People who are genuinely seeking deliverance know what I'm talking about. You can go through stages in receiving deliverance. Sometimes deliverance is all at once but sometimes it in layers because you are uncovering things that happened, things that got in you that you didn't even realize were there, either because you forgot them, or they were so subtle that you didn't even think they were sin. Or, if there was sin, we somehow think because we are not dead, **physically**, that God just forgot it. Not the case.

In getting your deliverance, you're not expecting someone to just fix it by suddenly laying hands on you, so you can go back to doing exactly what you were doing before. No! A big part of your deliverance is who you were when you entered into evil covenants, and soul ties. Your deliverance depends on who you are today, what you will honestly 'fess up to with a repentant heart with Godly sorrow. But it also depends on who you will be tomorrow in order to keep your deliverance by not entering into more evil covenants and becoming a reprobate with a seared conscience.

Well, God knows that if He just suddenly delivers a whole lot of folks, they will go back to exactly what they were doing before and create not just the same problem, but a problem that is seven times worse. That devil that was kicked out can't find any place to land, so it says it's going back to where it was and bringing seven more with it. And that problem will be far worse for the person who just got delivered --, even if that deliverance was only yesterday.

Then goeth he, and taketh with himself seven other spirits more wicked than himself, and they enter in and dwell there: and the last *state* of that man is worse than the first. Even so shall it be also unto this wicked generation. (Matthew 12:45)

Saints of God, this could be why it can be difficult to find a deliverance minister. Nobody wants to be responsible for a person who needs deliverance to end up with a worse problem than what they started out with. Saints of God, this is why we don't play around with deliverance, if you are not seriously seeking God, but only seeking relief, this may not end well. If you are not a saved, sanctified, set aside Protestant Christian, not dabbling in New Age and all other manner of blended and pagan religions, deliverance can make your situation far, far worse. That is if you even get delivered.

If a person is holding on to, hiding and harboring all kinds of idols and sins, a minister could spend hours and hours, days and days trying to get someone delivered, to no avail.

Again, after deliverance Jesus said, **Go and sin no more**. But if you don't know what a *sin is –, what is the use in getting delivered?*

You've Got the Ball

Therefore, there are things you have to do for yourself, yourself--, including repentance, no one can do it for you. And all of that is part of the *process* of you being changed on the inside—you becoming that new creation, that new man in Christ. **You** repent.

There are cases where we need the help of others. Sometimes in basketball you can just shoot the ball and it goes in the basket. Woo hoo! Sometimes you can do a layup and it goes in the basket; that's good, too. But when there is a lot of keen opposition on the basketball court, there are strategic plays such as the alley-oop where the ball is passed to a man in midair, and then the slam dunk. You can get that ball in the basket because you had help. Sometimes you need help to get your deliverance, but some things you do yourself.

If you haven't repented, let go of your idols, changed and really don't plan to change, then you will keep doing things the same way you've always done them, when you get the *ball*. Let's say it's a ball of cash, are you going to go shopping? Is that what got you in the financial trouble you were in in the first place? Are you going to go to the bar? Is that what got you into that alcohol trouble in the first place? Are you gonna go to the club, or are you going to go on multiple dates, when you get the ball – the ball of cash?

Repentance **changes** you.

What are you gonna do if you haven't changed? You are going to do the same things you've always done. You will get in the same trouble or far worse. God wants to hear your repentance; He loves a contrite spirit. So you might want to start your repentance now. Why wait for the last moment? Yes, repent for Heaven, repent for Eternity. But it is good that man repent and repent for <u>now</u> for an abundant, successful life here on Earth.

People who want deliverance start with repentance. There are so many people looking for deliverance; they may feel that their situation is dire, but they start with repentance. You will be amazed of what will drop off of you when you repent. You will start to get deliverance immediately. Until you reach full deliverance, start with repentance.

I know people who have been trying to get deliverance for years. And even if they find strong deliverance ministers, apostles, prophets, pastors, intercessors, et cetera, even then some *spirits* only come out by prayer and fasting. No one can fast for you and there are prayers that no one else can pray for you. Your own presence is required at the Court of Petition.

Some will only come out by resisting the devil and some will come out by change. Your changing. No one can resist the devil for you. No one can change *for* you; you must do that yourself.

Some who have been seeking deliverance a long time, not because they don't have spiritual help and deliverance ministers, it's that the person needs to change. They may need to change many things. Maybe the person needs to change only one thing. **My point is that repentance *may* take years** depending on many factors. **Repentance and change may take years.**

Yes, Jesus told the man on the Cross beside him that that man could be with Him in Paradise and that man repented then and was with Jesus. But the man was already on the cross – you're not on a cross, and you're not just hearing about Jesus for the first time, are you? Now might be a great time to start true repentance to the Lord. Don't wait until the last moment, while sinning right up to the last possible hour.

Living on the edge like that thinking that you can just have as much "*fun*" as you want right now and then you'll repent on the last day--, who knows when that is? This is not a game show where you try to beat the clock. We are talking about Eternity; it's too important to risk it with foolishness.

Even if the devil decides to back off for a day or two because of the power that the deliverance minister wields, *you* still have to **change** --, repent and change to get and keep your deliverance. If you choose to walk through the same minefield or field of mud over and again, you will continue to risk the same explosive moments or track the same dirt into your house. Your garments will be soiled all over again.

So, you might as well start true repentance now. People who really want deliverance start with repentance. The understanding and acknowledgement of what got you here and the choice to change, still may take years to reverse the mindset, the thought process, the addictive behavior. Men, people--, humans, get set in our ways. Evil comes in and it is determined to establish us in their evil pattern.

We must repent and change--, *ourselves*.

Your Soundtrack

I was in a business establishment the other day and a certain style of music was playing over the speakers. The owners of that business are probably good people. They may even be Christians, but they were playing worldly music. They may think it is innocent, after all, there were no cuss words in the lyrics.

But the thought came to me. How much of this music, this type of music will be in Heaven?

Will there be boom boxes in Heaven so people can make their own personal choice of music?

No.

How much of this music can even *get* into Heaven? How much of this secular music does **God** want to hear?

God doesn't like this music, or the lyrics. These lyrics are defiling. They soil the garments that should be pristine and white. They spoil the ears, minds, hearts, faith and expectations of the listeners. If this music is not going to be in Heaven and cannot be in Heaven, then where did *this* music come from?

I bring this up for a reason: Some people think there will be partying in hell. Of course there won't be. But they think that's where the *music* will be. The music will probably be there and maybe the creators of it as well. **There is no party and will be no party in hell.**

The music that they had growing up, while unregenerated, that they've grown up with, listened to, saturated in will not be taken to Heaven with you.

Is it going to stay on Earth, or go somewhere else?

I don't know.

I'm posing this question for you to consider just as I have been considering it.

Some people have made music into an idol—and feel they can't be a moment without this music playing in their ear. They can't be a moment without it playing in the atmosphere, playing in their cars and homes.

Sometimes there is NO SOUND in my house – no radio, tv, nothing – just quiet. Just pray, then listen to the Lord, or just *be*. Abide. Of course, I write a lot, so I am listening to the Holy Spirit, but quiet is my preference unless I'm praying or worshipping.

Some people come to my house, they like the atmosphere to a point, but then they complain that it's too quiet in here. There may be a constant noise and an uproar in their car, in their own houses, their workplaces, or just in their own ears—all the time. How do you hear God through all of that? Then I want to ask, with that idol of music or musicians in their **soul** how will they *get* into Heaven? That idol can't go in, and if you won't let go of the idol, how will *you* get into Heaven? Idolaters are people who have and serve idols.

Do you not know that the unrighteous will not inherit the kingdom of God? Do not be deceived. Neither fornicators, nor idolaters, nor adulterers, nor homosexuals, nor sodomites, nor thieves, nor covetous, nor drunkards, nor revilers, nor extortioners will inherit the kingdom of God. And such were some of you. But you were washed, but you were sanctified, but you were justified in the name of the Lord Jesus and by the Spirit of our God. (2 Corinthians 6:9-11

How long does repentance take--, repentance to become aware that you need to let go of a musical idol, or more than one, for example, and other things?

And if a person does get into Heaven, but they are really hooked on their music, and that music is **not** in Heaven, will they be miserable in Heaven? How many people in the Bible ran to, ran after, fought for, and fought over their idols?

How long does repentance take?

How long does it take to lose the *taste* for things of the world? Certainly not all in the last second of life!

And even in Heaven when they should be worshipping God, how will that transition happen, if that idol is still on the throne of your heart?

Oh, but I like to dance, you might be saying. Well good, dance unto the Lord. Dance in a way that's pleasing to Him. David danced before the Lord.

Being saved, but still having the taste for the world is somewhat akin to, or maybe hardly different than people who want certain medical situations to be fixed in their lives, but they don't want to have surgery. Some don't even want to go to a doctor. I'm not saying that a doctor is a deliverance minister in a spiritual sense, but in a physical sense things can be changed by medicines and doctors. So, many people will go to the pharmacy and get this, that or the other, or try concoctions or sometimes try wrong things completely. They want the things doctors can provide, but they don't want to go to the doctor. Lord, help us all.

Many people want the things of God but don't want to go *all in* while still trying to live on the edge, straddling two worlds to get what we think is the best of those two worlds. It doesn't work like that.

Some sick are trying in the physical to get deliverance from a malady, illness, sickness, discomfort, symptom, disease, or disorder without going to the doctor. In so doing, isn't there repentance such as a change of heart, and a change of behavior. If a person is smoking and drinking and it's affecting them in some way that they want to get healed from, first thing, stop drinking the beer or stop smoking the cigarettes, or at least cut down on intake. Well, that's a *form* of repentance. It's a physical repentance.

Repentance to God is **spiritual**, and it happens in your soul. When you are changed, your soul becomes different. By your repentance to God, you can be healed spontaneously by the Holy Spirit. You can be healed by the Word of God, if you but repent. The Word of God will bring your healing and transformation and your deliverance. So maybe you don't even need a deliverance minister if you just receive it and let it change you.

If you don't do anything, then your situation will be the same. When you stand in dirty water, won't mosquitoes be attracted to it? But when that water is flowing, moving and rolling across rocks—changing--, it becomes a living body of water. Mosquitoes and flies are far less than when the water is stagnant with scum and mold.

Without repentance nothing changes. So I ask again, How long do you think it'll take you to repent? Many who are seeking deliverance with or without a deliverance minister are studying the Word, praying the Word, meditating on the Word, getting the Word in their heart and realizing as they go along, *Oh, this happened in my life because of that.* And usually the *that* is something you did or something you allowed, something you accepted, something you chose.

Then as you continue or go deeper, then you realize, *Oh, I really must repent of that.* The Holy Spirit brings you to conviction, and you really must repent. Paul said he didn't realize he was a sinner until the Word was preached to him.

So when I'm asking how long does it take you to repent? Well, there are people who are trying to get deliverance from the *symptoms* of bad things, bad choices they've made. They've been trying to get deliverance for years. Evil comes in and it is determined to establish us in an evil pattern to keep us doing the same things, *or worse,* for our entire lives.

That's why people are still repenting two years later, three years later, 10 years later. If they keep seeking they will finally get the full deliverance from all of the layers of evil, the devil has been piling on when we were **not** serving God, not serving God properly, not serving God regularly. When we were serving our flesh, serving ourselves, chasing sin, chasing entertainment and *enjoyment* which led to sin chasing us.

A man chasing women, a man chasing money, chasing sex--, years, it can take years. So if it takes **years** to repent, what are you waiting for?

If you are determined to have a proper destination in the Kingdom of Heaven it is good that men repent, it is commanded. You can have the Kingdom now while here on Earth. It can happen.

Speaking of the music, there was a movie about certain music being the soundtrack to your life. **Is the music that you like the soundtrack to your *sins*?** The soundtrack to your youthful rebellion. Is it the soundtrack to your youthful lusts? The soundtrack to your partying and your dancing and staying up all night and disregarding, disrespecting your parents and being out in the streets?

So if you're in the Kingdom of God and you're seeking deliverance, for instance. Or you know or suspect you may need deliverance; don't you think you need to be delivered from the *soundtrack of your sin* as well as the sin itself? The soundtrack is part of it, and the lyrics of those sounds is another part of what influenced your thought life, which influenced your actions, which may have influenced your *sins*.

So if you're getting delivered from the things that you did years and possibly decades ago. Why do you think you can keep the *music*?

That music lulled, pulled you, or drove you like when Nebuchadnezzar says when you hear the music, **bow**. When you heard that soundtrack--, the soundtrack you *think* you created, you think you curated. You like this song. You like this artist. You like this band—it reminds you of—your days of sin. Come on, people.

All the while this music is directing you to *bow*. It's got words, it's got a driving beat, drumlines that can send a soul into a trance without them even knowing it.

The music is what helped lead you to these problems. It has a nice rhythm, a nice beat, a nice melody, pretty music, pretty lyrics. It takes you back *there* again. But, have you changed? Has your soul changed? Do you still want the same things; has your taste for the world not changed? After you get this deliverance allegedly or even after this repentance--, have you *changed*?

It Took Everything

All of your senses were employed to lure you into sin—you know, the sin that you are now being accused of in an Evil Petition.

Everything you saw, tasted, smelled, and heard--, all of your five senses, What you saw, heard, and what you felt. **All** of your 5 senses. You were lured, enticed, or dragged into sin. Maybe you were even *initiated* into something evil. And all that time, there was a soundtrack— all that music, it goes with that enticement, it goes with the luring, the drawing, the dragging, and the deception to get you to sin. So even if you repent and get your deliverance you go back to the *same music* that dragged you into the problem.

Things could be 7X worse; this is not wise.

If you are repentant and repenting to God regularly, let's say, daily--, there is a far less chance that an Evil Petition with your name on it is before the Court of Accusation because you and the Lord have already resolved this issue. You've taken the power out of the devil's hand because you've already repented, you've already owned up to it and you've already pleaded the Blood of Jesus.

But if you are a prideful person, stubborn or ignorant, you don't know that you should do this, or you don't repent, that is when the devil has something against you; he has something on you, and you may not even know that he has your name on a Docket in a Heavenly Court in the Court of Accusation to accuse you to get a judgement against you to start the stealing, the killing, or destroying of some part of your life, or even your whole life.

If you are full of pride, how will you hear God?

If you are playing the soundtrack of your old life, your slave life, of when you were in bondage and sin, and in Egypt, and you're playing the soundtrack—but you're free—free to do what? Do the same thing you did and lead yourself back into slavery and bondage? Trudging down the same road? How will you hear God? How will you hear? When He gives you signs and dreams or feelings or urgings:

THERE IS AN EVIL PETITION UP HERE in the COURT OF ACCUSATIONS AGAINST YOU.

If you are prideful and believe yourself to be so perfect you won't even ask God if there is an Evil Petition against you--, an Evil Petition that you must answer. And if you do get that far and get into the Heavenly Courts, don't get up there and be prideful and stupid. You repent. That's why you should repent now, **practice repentance** so when you are in Heavenly Courts you will repent with a quickness.

In that Court, the devil's accusation most likely is true. Then you ask that the Blood of Jesus speak for you, ask that the Blood of Jesus answer for you. Ask that your defense, the Blood of Jesus to blot out the sin and the iniquity; the

Blood of Jesus is your Defense, in the Name of Jesus.

You do not want to die, Accused--, that is, accused and unanswered. This is especially dangerous because the devil is bringing that evil petition before the Court of Accusation to get a judgment against you. The devil is after a judgment of ANY KIND against you, but don't you think he's hoping for death. Don't die accused. It is better to fall into the hands of an angry God, than in the hands of the devil or any of his evil human agents. Do not let an accusation stand unanswered by you.

The devil wants to steal from you, but that's not all he wants to do. Surely, he wants to do his worst; this way he can move on from you and pursue his next victim or victims.

Living this unrepentant life is full of self-deceit and lies, and PRIDE, if you think you'll get away with anything. What do you get away with? Most people want to get away with everything. But you don't get away with anything. Eyes are always on you, even evil eyes.

Ask to hear the accusation against you if it is not obvious that there is an accusation and that you know what it is. Guard your ears, you may be about to hear *anything* in that Court and you probably did it.

Accept the fact that what you hear may be <u>TRUE</u>, whether you remember it, or remember doing it or not; you are probably guilty.

God overlooked people's ignorance about these things in earlier times, but now he commands everyone everywhere to repent of their sins and turn to him. (Acts 17:30 NLT)

Therefore God overlooked *and* disregarded the *former* ages of ignorance; *but* now He commands all *people* everywhere to repent [that is, to change their old way of thinking, to regret their past sins, and to seek God's purpose for their lives], (Acts 17:30 AMP)

The devil is in God's court filing charges, if you don't show up, you forfeit and the devil wins his Evil Petition against you, because you're probably – no you *ARE* guilty. We have all sinned and fallen short, except for Jesus Christ, He is the only one without sin.

Oh no, not me!

Yes, you. you can sin with your thoughts, your words, your actions, those eyes – what they are roaming about looking at. You can sin with your whole body or just parts of it.

Not me – uh huh, you, me --, any of us.

Were *Those* Really Sins?

1. Evil thoughts and thoughts of sin are sin.
2. Evil words, including vows, oaths and curses are sin.
3. Evil Deeds are transgressions.
4. Through those eyes, looking on sin, pornography, lust, spying out another's liberties--, it's all sin.
5. The whole body can sin.

In this list of sins you may not even recognize some of them as sins, but hopefully, many of them, you will. Accusing the brethren, especially false accusations, adultery, anger, arrogance, bitterness, blasphemy, boasting, brutality, taking a brother to court, carousing, clamor, complaining, conceit, coveting, cowardice, deceit, defrauding, denying Christ, desiring praise of men, disobedience, divisions, drinking parties, drunkenness, not acknowledging our sins, afraid of people or circumstances, afraid to confess Jesus to people.

Being anxious, worrying. Envy, evil thoughts, false witnessing, fathers provoking their children. Filthiness, fleshliness, foolishness, fornication, greed, lust, lusting, haters of God, homosexuality, hypocrisy, idolatry, immorality, impurity, jealousy, jesting, judging, knowing to do good, but not doing it. Laying up treasures on earth. Legal matters, living for pleasure. Lovers of self. Malice, murder, murmuring, pride, prostitution, quarrels, reviling dignities, sensuality, slander, sorcery, speaking against the Holy Spirit, stealing, strife, swearing an oath, swindling, treachery, unbelief, unforgiveness, ungodliness, ungratefulness, unholiness, unrighteousness, wickedness, wrath, filthiness, Assault. Astrology. Backbiting. Refusing to be baptized. Baptized before believing in Jesus. Leading the blind astray. Eating blood. Being against a child of God. Causing a child to sin, deceiving a child of God. Despising a child of God. Enticing a child through lust.

Judging God's servant. Lying in wait to accuse someone. A false balance. Not helping those in the kingdom of God who are in need. Persecuting a child of God.

Some of these things seem so simple, yet they are things you can get called into Court for and an Evil Petition can come up against you. The devil is a legalist, a stickler for details. He will take anything, anything at all, no matter how small it seems, and will find any reason to take you to Court.

I believe that David knew about this Court and repented before God quickly, easily, and he learned to repent often. Psalm 51, pray that if you don't know how to repent, or what to say.

Psalm 51

Have mercy on me, O God,
according to your unfailing love;
according to your great compassion
blot out my transgressions.
² Wash away all my iniquity
and cleanse me from my sin.

³ For I know my transgressions,
and my sin is always before me.
⁴ Against you, you only, have I sinned
and done what is evil in your sight;
so you are right in your verdict
and justified when you judge.
⁵ Surely I was sinful at birth,
sinful from the time my mother conceived
me.
⁶ Yet you desired faithfulness even in the womb;
you taught me wisdom in that secret place.
⁷ Cleanse me with hyssop, and I will be clean;
wash me, and I will be whiter than snow.
⁸ Let me hear joy and gladness;
let the bones you have crushed rejoice.
⁹ Hide your face from my sins
and blot out all my iniquity.
¹⁰ Create in me a pure heart, O God,
and renew a steadfast spirit within me.
¹¹ Do not cast me from your presence
or take your Holy Spirit from me.
¹² Restore to me the joy of your salvation
and grant me a willing spirit, to sustain me.
¹³ Then I will teach transgressors your ways,
so that sinners will turn back to you.
¹⁴ Deliver me from the guilt of bloodshed, O
God,
you who are God my Savior,
and my tongue will sing of your

righteousness.
¹⁵ Open my lips, Lord,
and my mouth will declare your praise.
¹⁶ You do not delight in sacrifice, or I would
bring it;
you do not take pleasure in burnt offerings.
¹⁷ My sacrifice, O God, is a broken spirit;
a broken and contrite heart
you, God, will not despise.
¹⁸ May it please you to prosper Zion,
to build up the walls of Jerusalem.
¹⁹ Then you will delight in the sacrifices of the
righteous,
in burnt offerings offered whole;
then bulls will be offered on your altar.
Amen.

You are not repenting to the accuser, not to the one who's bringing the Evil Petition and seeking judgment to do you in.

David, who was talking to God, said, Against you *only* have I sinned. We repent to God, not to the accuser.

Once in this High Court we **ask for the hidden documents. Ask what the devil has on you.** We make friends with books; God keeps careful records. The counterfeit, the devil keeps records as well.

In Court we must respond to the accusation, and the answer is always the same. **The accusations are true.**

Vindication in the Courts of Heaven comes by **the Blood of Jesus; it is the only thing that will exonerate us**, take away our guilt and make us righteous again before the Righteous Judge, and set us free.

Jesus is our Great Advocate; He is our attorney. The Blood of Jesus is our defense. *Agree with your adversary quickly. NEVER DISPUTE AN ACCUSATION in the Court. We agree with the accusation and move on with the next part of the process.*

From here we need to remove the effect of the sin: we do this by acknowledging that the Blood of Jesus is your defense. Amen.

We need to also renounce agreement with evil vows, oaths, and words and let the Blood of Jesus be your defense.

Old oaths and vows can be very damaging. Many were made under strong emotions, in a defensive mode and/or in ignorance and can be internalized and even forgotten. Such are childhood vows and oaths, but these **are LEGAL contracts that can be used by whomever you made that soul tie with when you made that evil vow. There is a soul tie with** whatever *idol* you made that contract or covenant with – even unknowingly. You've got to break that. You've got to renounce it.

If the accusation involves parents, grandparents, ancestors, satanism, witchcraft, freemasonry, human slavery, human trafficking, **repent** on behalf of whomever it involves—, with a quickness.

If that accused person that caused the accusation against you is NOT you, but a relative or distant ancestor, you can't just have it thrown out saying, *It wasn't me, I didn't do it*. You can't just have it thrown out because it is too old or you don't know the original sinner/offender. It's in your bloodline. You also need to **forgive** your ancestor for this.

LOVE covers a multitude of sins. You need to love your ancestors, no matter what they did. Love is the hardest working SPIRITUAL FRUIT in my opinion, Amen. And it is the greatest; it covers a multitude of sins.

If you really want to get close to God – you've got to go through the Courts first. Sometimes those courts are in worship and praise --, courts of Thanksgiving, the Outer Court, Inner Court and the Holy of Holies. Sometimes it is an actual spiritual Court in the Heavenlies. You've got to go through Courts, that is spend time with God, that is, *court* God and love on Him.

In the Old Testament folks brought a sin offering. They came through the gates with Thanksgiving and when they got to the Inner Court, they had a sin offering, indicating their repentance. So, to get into the Heavenly Courts you should come repentant. But if you haven't, while you're there, repent.

Our natural court system is based on the spiritual courts of the LORD. It is modeled by what is in Heaven. Recall how God told Moses to set up a system so the peoples' complaints could be heard? Yes, let it be done on Earth as it is in Heaven.

Now it's time in this Heavenly Court to ask God for the verdict that <u>you</u> want: Ask Him to declare you **NOT GUILTY** by reason of the Blood of Jesus, which is your defense. It says in the Book of James that we have not because we ask not.

Now it's time to receive the Verdict from the Righteous Judge. You've confessed your sin and repented. Quietly, take a minute and listen. By the Blood of Jesus, which is your Defense, you are now: **NOT GUILTY.** Hallelujah!

But you had to show up there to make this happen.

Whatever symptoms, sickness, issues you were experiencing before, this **NOT GUILTY** verdict stops, erases, eradicates symptoms, sickness, disease, disorders, pain, poverty, lack, whatever you're going through that is definitely not of God. Now that you are declared **NOT GUILTY** these problems should lift from your life right away. These issues should release immediately, so you want to go to this Court. AMEN!

All other demonic activities against you should be GONE right away. For harassing *familiar spirits, spirit spouse* – ASK THE LORD FOR A DECREE OF DIVORCE against *spirit spouse* and *familiar spirits*. And hold on to that document, spiritually speaking.

If your Court of Heaven case is related to a court case in the natural, ask for a favorable outcome to that pending case as well.

As in the natural court, if you don't show up, you lose. PERIOD. It's automatic. So SHOW UP.

If you lose, then a bench warrant is issued (of sorts). Who's coming to enforce that bench warrant, who (what) is coming to get you? Satan's henchmen: demons and devils will come to steal, kill, and destroy, torment, disappoint, take things from you, frustrate your successes. Because really they want to throw you in jail, lock you up, put you in captivity, and steal from you, afflict you, torment you; they want to do their worst to you.

But you know that you have been declared **NOT GUILTY**. And if they continue to harass you, you may have to go back to Court and declare contempt of Court and let the Righteous Judge know that these spirits are not obeying the verdict that the Judge gave which declared that I am, you are: **NOT GUILTY**.

Jesus said to the people that He healed, *"Go and sin no more."* So we cannot use Grace as an opportunity to sin either, because we now know that we can go up to the Court and be let off by the Blood of Jesus; we don't do that. Having fully repented, you have been *changed* and you have lost your taste for the things of the world. Amen.

This is how you maintain your deliverance: we Go and we Sin No More--, as much as it is in us by help of the Holy Spirit. **NOT GUILTY**. Thank You, Lord.

Ask the Lord to change you back to your former glory. Ask Him to change you back to your pre-sin glory. *Lord, change me back to my pre-sin Glory. Amen.*

Recap

Demons can be stubborn and you may have to enforce the verdict you've received. If the enemy keeps harassing you by tempting you, for example, then you've got to stand your ground in prayer, making decrees and declarations. Some harassment is bombarding you with tempting thoughts to try to drag you back into evil patterns of sin, even though you've repented and changed.

YOU MUST RESIST. You may have to go back to Court to enforce the verdict; ask the Holy Spirit always to guide you.

Here are the steps again:

Worship the Lord. Repent. enter into prayer, repent, and wait on the Lord.

1. Go into the Spirit realm.

2. Ask the Judge to convene the Court.
3. Ask that your Accuser(s) appear.
4. Ask to hear the accusation against you. If these accusations are recorded in a book, ask that that book be presented or any hidden documents be produced.
5. Fear Not.
6. AGREE with the accusation.
7. State that Jesus is your Advocate and the Blood of Jesus is your defense.
8. Ask for a verdict from the Righteous Judge
9. Ask for all supporting documents.
10. If necessary, be prepared to enforce the Verdict against stubborn *spirits* that may keep harassing you.

The following prayers are prayers for NOW, they are NOT what you say in the Courts of Heaven. The preceding in this book has clearly outlined what you say in the Courts of Heaven. Follow the above protocol when you go to the Court of Accusation to answer an Evil Petition against you. God's Grace and Mercy to you, by the Blood of Jesus, Amen.

PRAYERS

By the Blood of Jesus I terminate all evil petitions up against my life in the Name of Jesus.

Lord, shine Your light on the enemy's schemes, plans and petitions up against me, in the Name of Jesus.

By the Blood of Jesus I command every hidden plan of darkness to be exposed and revealed.

I prophesy divine revelation and discernment in my life, in the Name of Jesus.

I speak against every form of deception and manipulation, in Jesus' Name.

I proclaim the light of God's truth to shine brightly in every situation in my life, in the Name of Jesus.

I decree and declare that my spiritual eyes and understanding are opened to recognize the schemes of the enemy.

Lord, let my ears be open to hear the voice of the Lord and to hear the Holy Spirit. Lord, let me walk in Wisdom and discernment, guided by the Holy Spirit and being sensitive to His leading, in the Name of Jesus.

Why sit we here until we die? Lord do not let me miss any evil strategies, plans or wickedness of the wicked one. Lord, do not let me miss any Petition up against me in any divine and spiritual Court, in the Name of Jesus.

Lord, let me know, let me **go** up to the Heavenly Courts and let me plead my case, in the Name of Jesus.

Lord let me defend myself, with Jesus as my Advocate and let the Blood of Jesus defend me, and answer for me, in the Name of Jesus.

Father, let every hidden plan of darkness, every accusation, even false accusations, let every Evil Petition before any Court of Heaven be exposed, and let me know about it, in the Name of Jesus.

Lord, let the Light of Your Truth shine brightly on every situation. Lord, let this mind be in me that was also in Christ Jesus and let it be renewed by Your Wisdom, knowledge and guided by the Holy Spirit, in the Name of Jesus.

Lord, I trust in You with all my heart and I no longer only lean on my own understanding or on the knowledge of men.

Lord, thank You for the Spirit of Wisdom and revelation so that I will know You better.

Let me hear or see if my name is on a spiritual Court Docket for an accusation that I should answer --that I **must** answer, in the Name of Jesus.

Through the Blood of Jesus I prophesy clarity and understanding in discerning the times--, discerning the seasons, in the Name of Jesus.

I receive spiritual insight and revelation in my life. I proclaim sharpening of my spiritual senses to recognize the voice of God to discern against truth versus deception.

I need Your Holy Spirit for guidance, revelation in every part of my life in Jesus' Name. Amen.

Lord, I know the enemy is constantly seeking whom he may devour. I know he is inciting, enticing, urging man to sin, Lord, don't let me be deceived, in the Name of Jesus.

Lord, forgive all disobedience, rebellion and sin, in the Name of Jesus.

In the Name of Jesus, I command every hidden agenda of the devil to be exposed against me and dismantled. I prophesy divine discernment and spiritual insight to know and discern the strategies of the enemy, in the Name of Jesus.

Lord, where I have fallen or fallen short and there is a heavenly case against me, LORD I shall appear; do not let the devil have judgment against me after the order of Job or others in Biblical, historical, and modern-day times, in the Name of Jesus.

Lord, if I am wearing a filthy robe of sin, have Your mighty angels to remove it and give me the robes of righteousness in Christ Jesus, Amen.

I bind every web of deceit created to entangle me, in the Name of Jesus.

Lord, unravel every lie and deception in the Name of Jesus.

Lord, I decree and declare that I am discerning and wise, walking in the light of God's revelation. Lord, I seek Your Word, Your Wisdom, Your knowledge, Your Face, Your grace so that I am not ignorant of the devil's devices and plans against me, in the Name of Jesus--, even in the Spirit, even in Heavenly Courts, in Jesus' Name.

Lord, by Your Spirit and the Blood of Jesus, let me overcome every trick and enemy scheme, in the Name of Jesus.

The LORD has established His Throne in the heavens and His kingdom rules over all. I affirm, Lord that you are Ruler over every wicked scheme and plan of the adversary. Let the enemy's Evil Petitions against me come to nothing, in the Name of Jesus.

You, Lord, are the Alpha and the Omega, the beginning and the end. Nothing can escape Your knowledge and control. Lord, do not let my enemies have dominion over me, in the Name of Jesus.

Lord, let no weapon formed against me prosper, by the power in the Blood of Jesus.

Lord, You are Sovereign God, let no weapon formed against me prosper, by the power in the Blood of Jesus.

Lord, You are Sovereign God, let no scheme of the enemy prosper against me, in the Name of Jesus.

I decree and declare that every wicked scheme, every wicked plot, or plan that the adversary has orchestrated, plotted, planned, enchanted or schemed against me is nullified by the power in the Blood of Jesus, AMEN.

Lord, give me godly thoughts to make godly decisions, in the Name of Jesus.

I bring every thought that exalts itself against the knowledge of God – I bring it down, in the Name of Jesus.

Lord, give me divine clarity against the enemy of my soul, in the Name of Jesus.

Lord, do not let me be too busy to hear You.

Do not let me be too sleepy to hear You.

Do not let me be too hungry to hear You.

Do not let me be too angry, confused, worried or frustrated to hear You, in the Name of Jesus.

Do not let me be too rushed, or distracted to sit and wait on You, Lord, in the Name of Jesus.

I bind every work of the flesh that is working against my Christian walk, in the Name of Jesus.

I speak against every demonic assignment aimed at my life, in the Name of Jesus.

Lord, I bind all sneakiness and stealth of the enemy that is working against me, in the Name of Jesus.

LORD, EXPOSE them, in Jesus' Name.

Lord, disrupt their networks of evil working against me and my life, in the Name of Jesus.

Lord, foil every wicked plan of the enemy against me, in the Name of Jesus.

Where I must step up and step in, Lord, let me do it. I will do it, in the Name of Jesus. By the authority in the Name of Jesus and by the power in the Blood of Jesus, I declare divine interference and divine disruption of every plot against my life, in the Name of Jesus.

I rebuke every tactic and assignment of darkness that seeks to steal, kill or destroy me or anything in my life that I have stewardship over.

HOUSEHOLD WITCHCRAFT – stand down, stand down or incur the wrath of GOD, in the Name of Jesus.

Because of these prayers, I bind up every retaliatory, vengeful, payback demon, in the Name of Jesus. I bind and paralyze you from working against me and my prayers, in the mighty Name of Jesus Christ.

I seal these declarations across every realm, dimension, age, and timeline, past present and future to infinity – I seal them with the Blood of Jesus and by the Holy Spirit of Promise, in the Name of Jesus.

Other books by this author

AK: The Adventures of the Agape Kid

AMONG SOME THIEVES

Churchzilla, T*he Wanna-Be, Supposed-to-be Bride of Christ*

Courtroom Prayers @Midnight

Demons Hate Questions

Don't Refuse Me, Lord (4 book series)

Evil Petition in the Court of Accusation

Evil Touch

The Fold (4 book series)

     The Fold (Book 1)

     Name Your Seed (Book 2)

     The Poor Attitudes of Money (Book 3)

     Do Not Orphan Your Seed

got HEALING? Verses for Life

got LOVE? Verses for Life

got money?

How to Dental Assist

Let Me Have A Dollar's Worth

Man Safari, *The*

Marriage Ed. *Rules of Engagement & Marriage*

Made Perfect in Love

Power Money: Nine Times the Tithe

The Power of Wealth *(forthcoming)*

Seasons of Grief

Seasons of War *(forthcoming)*

The Spirit of Poverty *(forthcoming)*

Triangular Power *(series)*

    Powers Above

    SUNBLOCK

    Do Not Swear by the Moon

    STARSTRUCK

Warfare Prayers Against Beauty Curses

Warfare Prayer Against Poverty

When the Devourer is Rebuked

The Wilderness Romance *(3-book series)*

    The Social Wilderness

    The Sexual Wilderness

Journals & Devotionals by this author:

The Cool of the Day – Journal for times with God

He Hears Us, Prayer Journal in 4 different colors

I Have A Star, Dream Journal kids, teen, adult

I Have A Star, Guided Prayer Journal, Boy or Girl

J'ai une Etoile, Journal des Reves

Let Her Dream, Dream Journal in multiple colors

Men Shall Dream, Dream Journal, (blue or black)

My Favorite Prayers (multiple covers)

My Sowing Journal (in three different colors)

Tengo una Estrella, Diario de Sueños

Wise Counsel (Journal in 2 styles)

Illustrated children's books by this author:

Be the Lion (3-book series)

Big Dog (8-book series)

Do Not Say That to Me